Wine Gift Baskets Business Book for Men for Women

Gift Basket Ideas to Get You the Massive Money You Want!

By

Brian Mahoney

Copyright © 2016 Brian Mahoney

All rights reserved.

ABOUT THE AUTHOR

Brian Mahoney is the author of over 100 business start-up guides, real estate investing programs and Christian literature. He started his company MahoneyProducts in 1992.

He served in the United States Army and worked over a decade for the United States Postal Service. An active real estate investor, he has also served as a minister for the Churches of Christ in Virginia and Michigan.

He has a degree in Applied Science and Information Technology with a specialty in Computer Programming with expertise in Java, C++ and C programming languages. Also, he is currently finishing an additional degree in Business Administration.

With the help of online businesses he has helped thousands of people all over the world start there own successful business.

http://www.briansmahoney.com/

Table of Contents
http://goo.gl/bzGp1n (Video Home Study Course)

Gift Basket Business Ideas

Making Massive Money with Gift Baskets

Fruit Bouquet * Corporate Gift Baskets * Baby Gift Baskets

Wine Gift Baskets * Candy Gift Baskets

I. Zero Cost Marketing

II. How Absolutely Anyone Can Start a Business Right This Second

III. Selecting The Right Business Name

IV. Business Tax Advantages

V. Money For Your Business - Up To $750,000 Guaranteed!

VI. MicroLoans

VII. EMPLOYEES

VIII. LOCATION

IX. BUSINESS POWER POINTS

X. WEB-RESOURCE GUIDE

GIFT BASKET BUSINESS IDEAS

Start-up cost: $5,000 - $15,000

Potential earnings: $25,000 - $50,000

Typical fees: Baskets are individually priced depending on the contents usually $35-$100 per basket; tailor-made baskets could be priced as high as $350 each.

Advertising: Zero Cost Online Marketing. Local newspapers, fliers, bulletin boards, direct mail to busy executives, , online classifieds, website

Qualifications: Natural creativity

Equipment needed: Baskets, filer, and gift materials, glue gun, shrink wrap machine , tables/counters for assembly, vehicle

Home business potential: Yes

Staff required: No, but it might be a good idea during the holiday seasons of Christmas, Easter and Valentine's Day

Hidden Costs: Shipping costs/vehicle expenses; you may need a liquor license if your baskets contain wine or champagne

Making Massive Money With Gift baskets

Finding the "perfect gift" for a special occasion is, for many people, can be very difficult. Running around from store to store only to find high priced or bad quality items can make gift giving very frustrating. When it comes to gift giving it's always a good idea to put some thought into the gift and match a good gift for the person. Gift baskets make it easy to match a gift to a person's taste. That is what makes the gift basket business so amazing.

Gift-giving isn't just a seasonal obligation. -- There's always a holiday on the horizon. Many people are becoming more proactive by creating affordable, unique gift ideas. These gift givers have discovered the exciting business of custom-made and often Gourmet Gift Baskets.

GIFT BASKETS

A gift basket, or fruit basket is typically a gift delivered to the recipient at their home or workplace. A variety of gift baskets exist: some contain fruit; while others might contain dry or canned foods such as tea, crackers and jam; or the basket might include a combination of fruit and dried good items. Gourmet gift baskets typically include exotic fruit, and often include quality cheese and wine, as well as other nonfood items.

FRUIT BOUQUET

A fruit bouquet is a fruit arrangement in the form of bouquet. The fruit is cut in the shape of flowers and leaves, and is arranged in the container with the help of sticks. A complete arrangement looks like a bouquet of flowers. Typically, a fruit bouquet is delivered to the recipient at their home or workplace.

Often these bouquets will be made to suit the recipients' needs, such as diabetic, vegan, vegetarian, gluten intolerance or wheat intolerance. Common fruit bouquet items include apples, artichokes, avocados, bananas, cheeses, grapes, lychees, mangoes, oranges, papayas, pineapples, pomegranates, strawberries, and Chocolates.

Often a gift basket will have a theme, such as for an occasion, like Christmas, Easter, Mother's Day, Father's Day, Thanksgiving, graduation, birthday, anniversary, baby shower, housewarming, or Valentine's Day. One can also send a sympathy gift basket or get well gift basket. A basket can be made to suit the dietary restrictions of the recipient, such as diabetic, peanut allergy, vegan, vegetarian, gluten or wheat intolerance.,

Corporate Gift Baskets

Many Corporate entities such as law firms, accounting, insurance, financing and banking, Medical and Pharmaceutical industries send higher end gift baskets for important clients to say 'thank you' for your business. Gifting is an important gesture in showing appreciation and confidence.

Baby Gift Baskets

The addition of a new member to a family is both an exciting and challenging time. Many people feel that sending a gift basket is the best way to express ones excitement and congratulations on the new little bundle of joy. Common items found in baby gift baskets include onesies, teethers, sleepers, rattles, plush stuffies, socks, wash cloths – all things the new parents will find very useful as they adjust to life with their new baby.

Wine Gift Baskets

There are plenty of wine lovers out there. That's why wine gift baskets can make the perfect gift. But creating them can be expensive. So below you have a list composed by Forbes Magazine of the top 19 great tasting wines that you can purchase for about twenty dollars!

1. Filipa Pato Rosé 'Metodo Tradicional' sparkling wine, Bairrada, Portugal, $15.

2. 2012 Domaine Wachau, Riesling Federspiel Terrassen, Austria $18

3. 2011 Garbó Negre, Spain, $19.

4. 2012 Campo Viejo Garnacha Rioja, Spain, $19.

5. 2011 La Quercia Montepulciano d'Abruzzo, Italy, $12.

6. 2008 La Valentina Spelt, Italy, $20.

7. 2012 Sofia Chardonnay, Monterey, CA, $19.

8. 2005 Beronia Reserva Rioja, Spain $20.

9. 2011 Thomas Goss Cabernet Sauvignon, Australia, $17.

10. 2012 Maison Joseph Drouhin Laforet Bourgogne Chardonnay, France, $18.

11. 2011 Inama 'Vin Soave' Soave Classico, Italy, $15.

12. 2012 Hogwash Rosé, CA, $15.99.

13. 2012 Terras Gauda Abadia de San Campio, Albarino, Rias Biaxas, Spain, $20.

14. 2009 Altolandon Rayuelo, Spain, $20.

15. 2010 Sobon Estate Zinfandel, Amador, CA, $17.

16. 2012 Santa Carolina Sauvignon Blanc, Chile, $12.99.

17. 2010 Ouled Thaleb Syrah, Morocco, $16.

18. 2012 Apaltagua Rosé of Carmenere, Central Valley, Chile, $12.

19. 2012 Allan Scott Pinot Noir, Marlborough, New Zealand, $14.99.

After you purchase your wine, you can add cheese and other tasty treats to your gift basket. You can add cheese bars, wedges of cheese, cheese spreads, chips, meat sticks or slim Jims, crackers, gourmet mustards, pretzels, hersheys dark chocolate, a cheese board and cheese knife.

Candy Gift Baskets

Candy gift baskets can offer the perfect sweet tooth cure for your family, friends and business associates. Here are some ideas for candy gift baskets.

Healthy Candy Ideas

1. Sugar-free candy bars: Hershey now has an entire line of sugar free candy bars that retail for about $3.00 a bag.

2. Flavanol-rich chocolate: Mars is coming out with a product that is high in flavanol, which is a type of anti-oxidant.

3. Fruit juice concentrate candies: Instructables has fruit juice gummy candies.

4. Diet candy: Many large makers are now offering a whole line of healthier candy which they are labeling as diet candy.

5. Apples, oranges and other fresh fruits: And, it never hurts to add to your candy gift basket a few pieces of whole fresh fruits such as apples, orange and raisins.

TOP SELLING CANDY IDEAS

According to Jane Wells a reporter for CNBC here is the top 5 candies in the world. The nice thing about this list is that the candies are easy to fine and are sold almost everywhere.

5. KitKat Bar

4. Hershey Bar

3. Snickers

2. M&Ms

1. Reese's

1. ZERO COST MARKETING

The web-RESOURCE guide has plenty of web sites for you to find products at huge dicounts. Below are a few steps to market those products using ZERO COST INTERNET MARKETING stratigies.

While there are many ways to market we are only going focuse on ZERO COST MARKETING. You are starting up. You can always go for the more expensive ways of marketing after your business is producing income.

FREE WEB HOSTING

Get a web site. You can get a free web site at weebly.com. Or just type "free web hosting" in a google, bing or yahoo search engine.

PAID WEB HOSTING

Free is nice, but you when you need to expand your business it is best to go with a paid web hosting service. There are several that give you good value for under $10.00 a month.

1. Yahoo small business
2. Intuit.com
3. ipage.com

Yahoo small business allows for unlimited web pages and is probably the best overall value, but they require a years payment up front. Intuit allows for monthly payments.

For free ecommerce on your web site, open up a Paypal account and get the HTML code for payment buttons for free. Then put those buttons on your web site.

Step by Step basic zero cost web site traffic instructions

Step 1 zero cost internet marketing

Now that your web site is up and running you should register it with at least the top 3 search engines. 1. Google 2. Bing 3. Yahoo.

Step 2 zero cost internet marketing

Write and submit a press release. Google "free press release sites" for press release sites that will allow you to summit press releases for free.

Step 3 zero cost internet marketing

Write and submit articles to article marketing web sites like ezinearticles.com.

Step 4 zero cost internet marketing

Create and submit videos to video sharing sites like dailymotion.com or youtube.com.

Step 5 zero cost internet marketing

Submit your web site to dmoz.org. This is a huge open directory that many smaller search engines go to get web sites for their database.

If you would like more detailed information on Zero Cost Marketing type the link below into your browser for a complete video training program...

http://goo.gl/bzGp1n

2. How Absolutely Anyone Can Start a Business Right This Second

The other day I was driving down a street in a commercial district and noticed a moving van. Two "blue collar workers" were busy loading office furniture in a company-owned vehicle. It was obvious that they were employees of this major company and I surmised they were making about $12 per hour.

I then thought about the normal lives these men probably lived. They had to punch a time-clock every day. If they were sick, they had to report to a boss and get permission to stay home. They had to depend on the company to pay them a weekly salary. They got paid the same amount of money every week and were lucky to get a raise every year or so.

Because of being controlled by a time clock at work, they naturally arranged their lives in the same fashion. They came home at the same time, ate dinner at the same time, looked forward to Friday for 2 days of rest but ended up cramming all their neglected responsibilities from the previous week into those 2 days.

The entire human race consists of two major groups of people: (1) Leaders and (2) Followers. Leaders have a built-in knack to not be happy with the normal flow of existence. Leaders are continually striving for a way out of this rat-race because they have a human characteristic of wanting to lead instead of follow.

But a good many of these leaders don't have a lot of money because they have been working for an employer all their lives. They recognize that they will never achieve the level of success they desire working for someone else. But they can't just leave their job and survive on their own. How could they pay the rent? Put their children through college? Buy the groceries? Pay Visa and Mastercard? With all these fears sitting in the leader will often exist as a follower because he or she doesn't believe they have a choice.

But they do! In fact, the answer is right under their noses. Allow me to explain . . .

Let's take the guy working for the moving company that I saw when I was driving down the street. He could offer the same service on weekends through word-of-mouth advertising. By placing a simple classified ad under Services Offered in the local newspaper, he could pick up a couple jobs a month and bring in an extra income.

Or how about the lady that just had a baby and wants to stay at home with it. Her maternity leave from her employer, only allows her 6 weeks. If she doesn't go back to work then she will either lose her job, her income or both. If her husband doesn't bring in enough money to support her and the baby she doesn't think she has a choice. The new mother will sacrifice money for her child.

But if this lady wants to stay at home with her child, why doesn't she start a home day-care center? That way, she would still make money and be able to be with her new child at the same time. Good for the child. Good for the mother. Good for the family unit. Good for other working mothers who can trust a "mother-run" day care center versus a commercial one. Plus since the day care center is in this mother's home, she can charge 40% to 50% less than commercial day care centers and probably make more money compared to her old job.

Too often, people who want to break out of the mold and start their own business will seek for products and services they know absolutely nothing about. Someone told them they could make a lot of money doing this and doing that. But the truth is that it will take anyone longer to make money with a product or service that they have to learn. In fact, this learning period could take a year or more. The person could easily be discouraged about a small business if it doesn't make any money by then.

So, if you are considering starting a small business; entertain the possibility of starting one based on the skills you already possess.

3. Selecting The Right Business Name

Ask 500 people already in business how they decided upon their business name and you will get 500 different answers. Everyone has a story behind how they chose their own business name. Even if the business is named after their own birth name, there's a reason why this was done.

When you open a business, in a sense, you are causing a new birth to begin. This new birth was created from an idea alone by you or your associates. It will have its own bank account, it's own federal identification number, it's own credit accounts, it's own income and it's own bills. On paper, it is another individual! Just as if you were choosing a name for your own unborn child, you need to spend considerable time in deciding upon your business name.

There are several reasons why a good business name is vitally important to your business. The first obvious reason is because it is the initial identification to your customers. No one would want to do business with someone if they didn't have a company name yet. This makes you look like an amateur who is very unreliable. Even if you call your company "Kevin's Lawn Service," a company name has been established and you are indeed a company. People will therefore feel more comfortable dealing with you.

Secondly, a business name normally is an indication as to the product or service you offer. "Mary's Typing Service," "Karate Club for Men," "Jim-Dandy Jack-of-all-Trades," "Laurie and Steve's Laundry," "Misty's Gift Boutique," and "Star 1 Publishers" are all examples of simple business names that immediately tell the customer what product you offer.

However, most people will choose the simple approach when naming their business. They use their name, their spouse's name, their children's names or a combination of these names when naming a business. The national hamburger-restaurant chain "Wendy's" was named after the owner's daughter.

However, research has proven that these "cutesy" names are not the best names to use for a business. Many experts claim that it makes the business look too "mom-and-pop-sie." However, this depends on the business. If you are selling something that demands this mood or theme to appeal to your market, it's best to use this approach.

Personally, I am inclined to name my businesses with catchy names that stick in people's heads after we have initially made contact. Names like, "Sensible Solutions," "Direct Defenders," "Moonlighters Ink," "Printer's Friend," "Strictly Class," "Collections and Treasures," and "Starlight on Twilight" are all good examples of catchy names. These types of names relate to your product or service but serve as a type of slogan for your business. This is a big help when marketing.

A friend I know owns a business called "Mint and Pepper." He grows and sells his own line of raw seasonings to people in the local area. At a get-together for small businesses, he passed out his business card. The card had a peppermint candy glued on the back and the slogan read: "Your business is worth a mint to us." This marketing concept not only got my friend noticed and remembered, but brought in several large orders for the business.

When you name a child, you may not decide upon a definite name until after they are born. You do this because a name is sometimes associated with a type of personality. When you name a business you may need to wait until you have a product or service to sell and then decide upon a business name before going into the business itself because your business name should give some clue as to what product or service you are selling.

A business named "Joe's Collections" normally wouldn't sell car parts and a business named "Charlie Horse" would not sell knitting supplies.

To generate ideas - begin looking at business signs everywhere you go. Notice which ones catch your eye and stick in your mind. Try and figure out "why" they stuck in your mind. Naturally, the business "Dominos Pizza" sticks in your mind because it is nationally known. These don't count!

Look around and notice the smaller businesses. Take your time. Within a few days you should be able to come up with a few potential business names.

Then, when you finally find a few names you really like - try reciting them to other people and get their opinion. It won't be long until your business will have the proper name that will carry it through it's life!

HINT:

Try to avoid very long names so they will fit into small display ads. Amalgamated International Enterprises can be easily presented as AIE - which is easier and shorter to spell.

Register Your Business Name

Naming your business is an important branding exercise, but if you choose to name your business as anything other than your own personal name then you'll need to register it with the appropriate authorities.

This process is known as registering your "Doing Business As" (DBA) name.

What is a "Doing Business As" Name?

A fictitious name (or assumed name, trade name or DBA name) is a business name that is different from your personal name, the names of your partners or the officially registered name of your LLC or corporation.

It's important to note that when you form a business, the legal name of the business defaults to the name of the person or entity that owns the business, unless you choose to rename it and register it as a DBA name.

For example, consider this scenario: John Smith sets up a painting business. Rather than operate under his own name, John instead chooses to name his business: "John Smith Painting". This name is considered an assumed name and John will need to register it with the appropriate local government agency.

The legal name of your business is required on all government forms and applications, including your application for employer tax IDs, licenses and permits.

Do I Need a "Doing Business As" Name?

A DBA is needed in the following scenarios:

Sole Proprietors or Partnerships – If you wish to start a business under anything other than your real name, you'll need to register a DBA so that you can do business as another name.
Existing Corporations or LLCs – If your business is already set up and you want to do business under a name other than your existing corporation or LLC name, you will need to register a DBA.
Note: Not all states require the registering of fictitious business names or DBAs.

How to Register your "Doing Business As" Name

Registering your DBA is done either with your county clerk's office or with your state government, depending on where your business is located. There are a few states that do not require the registering of fictitious business names.

4. Business Tax Advantages

Every year, several thousand people develop an interest in "going into business." Many of these people have an idea, a product or a service they hope to promote into an income producing business which they can operate from their homes.

If you are one of these people, here are some practical thoughts to consider before hanging out the "Open for Business" sign.

In areas zoned "Residential Only," your proposed business could be illegal. In many areas, zoning restrictions rule out home businesses involving the coming and going of many customers, clients or employees. Many businesses that sell or even store anything for sale on the premises also fall into this category.

Be sure to check with your local zoning office to see how the ordinances in your particular area may affect your business plans. You may need a special permit to operate your business from your home; and you may find that making small changes in your plan will put you into the position of meeting zoning standards.

Many communities grant home occupation permits for businesses involve typing, sewing, and teaching, but turn thumbs down on requests from photographers, interior decorators and home improvement businesses to be run from the home. And often, even if you are permitted to use your home for a given business, there will be restrictions that you may need to take into consideration. By all means, work with your zoning people, and save yourself time, trouble and dollars.

One of the requirements imposed might be off street parking for your customers or patrons. And, signs are generally forbidden in residential districts. If you teach, there is almost always a limit on the number of students you may have at any one time.

Obtaining zoning approval for your business, then, could be as simple as filling out an application, or it could involve a public hearing. The important points the zoning officials will consider will center around how your business will affect the neighborhood. Will it increase the traffic noticeably on your street? Will there be a substantial increase in noise? And how will your neighbors feel about this business alongside their homes?

To repeat, check into the zoning restrictions, and then check again to determine if you will need a city license. If you're selling something, you may need a vendor's license, and be required to collect sales taxes on your transactions. The sale tax requirement would result in the need for careful record keeping.

Licensing can be an involved process, and depending upon the type of business, it could even involve the inspection of your home to determine if it meets with local health and building and fire codes. Should this be the case, you will need to bring your facilities up to the local standards. Usually this will involve some simple repairs or adjustments that you can either do personally, or hire out to a handyman at a nominal cost.

Still more items to consider: Will your homeowner's insurance cover the property and liability in your new business? This must definitely be resolved, so be sure to talk it over with your insurance agent.

Tax deductions, which were once one of the beauties of engaging in a home business, are not what they once were. To be eligible for business related deductions today, you must use that part of your home claimed EXCLUSIVELY AND REGULARLY as either the principal location of your business, or place reserved to meet patients, clients or customers.

An interesting case in point: if you use your den or a spare bedroom as the principal place of business, working there from 8:00 to 5:00 every day, but permit your children to watch TV in that room during evening hours, the IRS dictates that you cannot claim a deduction for that room as your office or place of business.

There are, however, a couple of exceptions to the "exclusive use" rule. One is the storage on inventory in your home, where your home is the location of your trade or business, and your trade or business is the selling of products at retail or wholesale. According to the IRS, such storage space must be used on a REGULAR Basis, and be separately identifiable space.

Another exception applies to daycare services that are provided for children, the elderly, or physically or mentally handicapped. This exception applies only if the owner of the facility complies with the state laws for licensing.

To be eligible for business deductions, your business must be an activity undertaken with the intent of making profit. It's presumed you meet this requirement if your business makes a profit in any two years of a five-year period.

Once you are this far along, you can deduct business expenses such as supplies, subscriptions to professional journals, and an allowance for the business use of your car or truck. You can also claim deductions for home related business expenses such as utilities, and in some cases, even a new paint job for your home.

The IRS is going to treat the part of your home you use for business as though it were a separate piece of property. This means that you'll have to keep good records and take care not to mix business and personal matters. No specific method of record keeping is required, but your records must clearly justify and deductions you claim.

You can begin by calculating what percentage of the house is used for business, Either by number of rooms or by area in square footage. Thus, if you use one of the five rooms for your business, the business portion is 20 percent. If you run your business out of a room that's 10 by 12 feet, and the total area of your home is 1,200 square feet, the business space factor is 10 percent.

An extra computation is required if your business is a home day care center. This is one of the exempted activities in which the exclusive use rule doesn't apply. Check with your tax preparer and the IRS for an exact determination.

If you're a renter, you can deduct the part of your rent which is attributable to the business share of your house or apartment. Homeowners can take a deduction based on the depreciation of the business portion of their house.

There is a limit to the amount you can deduct. This is the amount equal to the gross income generated by the business, minus those home expenses you could deduct even if you weren't operating a business from your home. As an example, real estate taxes and mortgage interest are deductible regardless of any business Activity in your home, so you must subtract from your business Gross income the percentage that's allocable to the business portion of your home. You thus arrive at the maximum amount for home-related business deductions.

If you are self-employed, you claim your business deductions on SCHEDULE C, PROFIT(or LOSS) for BUSINESS OR PROFESSION. The IRS emphasizes that claiming business-at-home deductions does not automatically trigger an audit on your tax return. Even so, it is always wise to keep meticulously within the proper guidelines, and of course keep detailed records if you claim business related expenses when you are working out of your home. You should discuss this aspect of your operation with your tax preparer or a person qualified in the field of small business tax requirements.

If your business earnings aren't subject to withholding tax, and your estimated federal taxes are $100 or more, you'll probably be filing a Declaration of Estimated Tax, Form 1040 ES. To complete this form, you will have to estimate your income for the coming year and also make a computation of the income tax and self-employed tax you will owe.

The self-employment taxes pay for Social Security coverage. If you have a salaried job covered by Social Security, the self-employment tax applies only to that amount of your home business income that, when added to your salary, reaches the current ceiling. When you file your Form 1040-ES, which is due April 15, you must make the first of four equal installment payments on your estimated tax bill.

Another good way to trim taxes is by setting up a Keogh plan or an Individual Retirement Account. With either of these, you can shelter some of your home business income from taxes by investing it for your retirement.

5. Money For Your Business - Up To $750,000 Guaranteed!

Roughly 98 percent of the companies in the United States qualify as small businesses - and most of these businesses are eligible for U.S. Small Business Administration loans up to $750,000, available to build their operations.

To these businesses, the SBA guarantees of 90 percent on lenders loans up to $155,000 and guarantees of 85 percent on larger loans. The SBA even makes direct loans to eligible individuals and companies.

As with any business loan, the SBA and its associated lenders look at the applicant's personal credit history, the business financial profile and management experience, and the growth trends in the applicant's industry.

Among SBA objectives are greater support for women and minorities in business, aid to rural small business development, and urban business and job creation programs.

The 7 (a) loan guarantee program is the SBA's standard program. It aids small businesses needing funds to buy fixed assets or for working capital.

In the 8 (a) program, the SBA acts as prime contractor, contracting with other federal agencies to negotiate subcontracts with small businesses owned by socially or economically disadvantaged individuals.

In 1987, 370,000 companies in the U.S. were owned by Asians, American Indians and other minorities. The SBA made over 1600 loans totaling over $400 million to these companies.

There were more than 420,000 Black-owned business in the U.S. in 1987, up almost 40 % from 1982. The SBA made more than 500 loans and over 1600 8 (a) contracts totaling over $1.4 billion Black-owned companies in 1990.

Over 420,000 businesses were Hispanic-owned in 1987, up more than 80% since 1982. A number of these firms took part in SBA programs.

Disabled and Vietnam-era veterans who cannot secure business financing on reasonable terms from other sources can go to the SBA. Veterans can use these loans to start a small business, or to build an existing business.

Small companies in the field of energy conservation can find financial support in the SBA's Small Business Solar Energy and Conservation Loan Program. Loans are available to a broad range of companies seeking ways to cut use of U.S. energy resources.

The SBA's Small Loan program encourages SBA-guaranteed loans of $50,000 or less. Applicants should ask for the SBA Form 4 short form to apply for the small loans.

The recent microloan program offering loans of $200 to $15,000 makes SBA funding available to even tiny businesses.

The SBA HAL-1 and HAL-2 programs help handicapped individuals and non=profit workshops to establish, purchase or run a small businesses

The SBA's Certified Development Company (CDC) loan program offers credit for small and medium sized businesses that fall between the cracks of programs covered by traditional lenders. And the Export Revolving Line of Credit program helps small exporters to obtain an SBA guarantee on a loan or line of credit.

SBA LOANS AND GRANTS

http://www.sba.gov/category/navigation-structure/loans-grants/

6. MICROLOANS

Microloan Program

What is a Microloan?
The Microloan Program provides small, short-term loans to small business concerns and certain types of not-for-profit child-care centers. The SBA makes funds available to specially designated intermediary lenders, which are nonprofit community-based organizations with experience in lending as well as management and technical assistance. These intermediaries make loans to eligible borrowers. The maximum loan amount is $50,000, but the average microloan is about $13,000.

How Microloan Funds May Be Used
Microloans may be used for the following purposes:

Working capital
The purchase of inventory or supplies
The purchase of furniture or fixtures
The purchase of machinery or equipment.
Proceeds from a microloan cannot be used to pay existing debts or to purchase real estate.

Technical Assistance
Each intermediary (lender) is required to provide business training and technical assistance to its micro-borrowers. If you apply for microloan financing, you may be required to fulfill training and/or planning requirements before your loan application is considered. This business training can be helpful to you as you launch or expand your small business.

Terms, Interest Rates, and Fees
Loan terms vary according to:

The size of the loan
The planned use of funds
The requirements of the intermediary lender
The needs of the small business borrower
The maximum term allowed for a microloan is six years. Interest rates vary, depending on the intermediary lender and costs to the intermediary from the U.S. Treasury. Generally, these rates will be between 8 and 13 percent.

Collateral
Each intermediary lender has its own lending and credit requirements. Generally, intermediaries require some type of collateral as well as the personal guarantee of the business owner.

Contact Your Local Microloan Intermediary
Small businesses interested in applying for a microloan should contact an intermediary in their area, since all credit decisions are made on the local level. The Microloan Program is available in selected locations in most states. For more information contact your local SBA District Office or review the attached file for a list of participating intermediaries by state.

7. EMPLOYEES

Hire Your First Employee
If your business is booming, but you are struggling to keep up, perhaps it's time to hire some help.

The eight steps below can help you start the hiring process and ensure you are compliant with key federal and state regulations.

Step 1. Obtain an Employer Identification Number (EIN)

Before hiring your first employee, you need to get an employment identification number (EIN) from the U.S. Internal Revenue Service. The EIN is often referred to as an Employer Tax ID or as Form SS-4. The EIN is necessary for reporting taxes and other documents to the IRS. In addition, the EIN is necessary when reporting information about your employees to state agencies. Apply for EIN online or contact the IRS at 1-800-829-4933.

Step 2. Set up Records for Withholding Taxes

According to the IRS, you must keep records of employment taxes for at least four years. Keeping good records can also help you monitor the progress of your business, prepare financial statements, identify sources of receipts, keep track of deductible expenses, prepare your tax returns, and support items reported on tax returns.

Below are three types of withholding taxes you need for your business:

Federal Income Tax Withholding
Every employee must provide an employer with a signed withholding exemption certificate (Form W-4) on or before the date of employment. The employer must then submit Form W-4 to the IRS. For specific information, read the IRS' Employer's Tax Guide [PDF].

Federal Wage and Tax Statement

Every year, employers must report to the federal government wages paid and taxes withheld for each employee. This report is filed using Form W-2, wage and tax statement. Employers must complete a W-2 form for each employee who they pay a salary, wage or other compensation.

Employers must send Copy A of W-2 forms to the Social Security Administration by the last day of February to report wages and taxes of your employees for the previous calendar year. In addition, employers should send copies of W-2 forms to their employees by Jan. 31 of the year following the reporting period. Visit SSA.gov/employer for more information.

State Taxes

Depending on the state where your employees are located, you may be required to withhold state income taxes. Visit the state and local tax page for more information.

Step 3. Employee Eligibility Verification

Federal law requires employers to verify an employee's eligibility to work in the United States. Within three days of hire, employers must complete Form I-9, employment eligibility verification, which requires employers to examine documents to confirm the employee's citizenship or eligibility to work in the U.S. Employers can only request documentation specified on the I-9 form.

Employers do not need to submit the I-9 form with the federal government but are required to keep them on file for three years after the date of hire or one year after the date of the employee's termination, whichever is later.

Employers can use information taken from the Form I-9 to electronically verify the employment eligibility of newly hired employees by registering with E-Verify.

Visit the U.S. Immigration and Customs Enforcement agency's I-9 website to download the form and find more information.

Step 4. Register with Your State's New Hire Reporting Program

All employers are required to report newly hired and re-hired employees to a state directory within 20 days of their hire or rehire date. Visit the New Hires Reporting Requirements page to learn more and find links to your state's New Hire Reporting System.

Step 5. Obtain Workers' Compensation Insurance

All businesses with employees are required to carry workers' compensation insurance coverage through a commercial carrier, on a self-insured basis or through their state's Workers' Compensation Insurance program.

Step 6. Post Required Notices

Employers are required to display certain posters in the workplace that inform employees of their rights and employer responsibilities under labor laws. Visit the Workplace Posters page for specific federal and state posters you'll need for your business.

Step 7. File Your Taxes

Generally, employers who pay wages subject to income tax withholding, Social Security and Medicare taxes must file IRS Form 941, Employer's Quarterly Federal Tax Return. For more information, visit IRS.gov.

New and existing employers should consult the IRS Employer's Tax Guide to understand all their federal tax filing requirements.

Visit the state and local tax page for specific tax filing requirements for employers.

Step 8. Get Organized and Keep Yourself Informed

Being a good employer doesn't stop with fulfilling your various tax and reporting obligations. Maintaining a healthy and fair workplace, providing benefits and keeping employees informed about your company's policies are key to your business' success. Here are some additional steps you should take after you've hired your first employee:

Set up Record keeping

In addition to requirements for keeping payroll records of your employees for tax purposes, certain federal employment laws also require you to keep records about your employees. The following sites provide more information about federal reporting requirements:

Tax Recordkeeping Guidance

Labor Recordkeeping Requirements

Occupational Safety and Health Act Compliance

Employment Law Guide (employee benefits chapter)

Apply Standards that Protect Employee Rights

Complying with standards for employee rights in regards to equal opportunity and fair labor standards is a requirement. Following statutes and regulations for minimum wage, overtime, and child labor will help you avoid error and a lawsuit. See the Department of Labor's Employment Law Guide for up-to-date information on these statutes and regulations.

Also, visit the Equal Employment Opportunity Commission and Fair Labor Standards Act.

8. Your Business Location

Choosing a business location is perhaps the most important decision a small business owner or startup will make, so it requires precise planning and research. It involves looking at demographics, assessing your supply chain, scoping the competition, staying on budget, understanding state laws and taxes, and much more.

Here are some tips to help you choose the right business location.

Determine Your Needs

Most businesses choose a location that provides exposure to customers. Additionally, there are less obvious factors and needs to consider, for example:

Brand Image – Is the location consistent with the image you want to maintain?

Competition – Are the businesses around you complementary or competing?

Local Labor Market – Does the area have potential employees? What will their commute be like?

Plan for Future Growth – If you anticipate further growth, look for a building that has extra space should you need it.
Proximity to Suppliers – They need to be able to find you easily as well.

Safety – Consider the crime rate. Will employees feel safe alone in the building or walking to their vehicles?
Zoning Regulations – These determine whether you can conduct your type of business in certain properties or locations. You can find out how property is zoned by contacting your local planning agency.

Evaluate Your Finances

Besides determining what you can afford, you will need to be aware of other financial considerations:

Hidden Costs – Very few spaces are business ready. Include costs like renovation, decorating, IT system upgrades, and so on.

Taxes – What are the income and sales tax rates for your state? What about property taxes? Could you pay less in taxes by locating your business across a nearby state line?

Minimum Wage – While the federal minimum wage is $8.50 per hour, many states have a higher minimum. View the Department of Labor's list of minimum wage rates by state.

Government Economic Incentives – Your business location can determine whether you qualify for government economic business programs, such as state-specific small business loans and other financial incentives.

Is the Area Business Friendly?

Understanding laws and regulations imposed on businesses in a particular location is essential. As you look to grow your business, it can be advantageous to work with a small business specialist or counselor. Check what programs and support your state government and local community offer to small businesses. Many states offer online tools to help small business owners start up and succeed. Local community resources such as SBA Offices, Small Business Development Centers, Women's Business Centers, and other government-funded programs specifically support small businesses.

The Bottom Line

Do your research. Talk to other business owners and potential co-tenants. Consult the small business community and utilize available resources, such as free government-provided demographic data, to help in your efforts.

9. BUSINESS POWER POINTS

10 Steps to Starting a Business

Starting a business involves planning, making key financial decisions and completing a series of legal activities. These 10 easy steps can help you plan, prepare and manage your business. Click on the links to learn more.

Step 1: Write a Business Plan

Use these tools and resources to create a business plan. This written guide will help you map out how you will start and run your business successfully.

Step 2: Get Business Assistance and Training

Take advantage of free training and counseling services, from preparing a business plan and securing financing, to expanding or relocating a business.

Step 3: Choose a Business Location

Get advice on how to select a customer-friendly location and comply with zoning laws.

Step 4: Finance Your Business

Find government backed loans, venture capital and research grants to help you get started.

Step 5: Determine the Legal Structure of Your Business

Decide which form of ownership is best for you: sole proprietorship, partnership, Limited Liability Company (LLC), corporation, S corporation, nonprofit or cooperative.

Step 6: Register a Business Name ("Doing Business As")

Register your business name with your state government.

Step 7: Get a Tax Identification Number

Learn which tax identification number you'll need to obtain from the IRS and your state revenue agency.

Step 8: Register for State and Local Taxes

Register with your state to obtain a tax identification number, workers' compensation, unemployment and disability insurance.

Step 9: Obtain Business Licenses and Permits

Get a list of federal, state and local licenses and permits required for your business.

Step 10: Understand Employer Responsibilities

Learn the legal steps you need to take to hire employees.

10. WEB RESOURCE GUIDE GIFT BASKETS SUPPLIES

As of the writting of this book(Aug 2016) all of the companies below, website is up and have an active business. From time to time companies go out of business. I have no control over that.

That is why instead of giving you just 1 source I have given you 12!

1. http://goo.gl/lvSY8G

2. http://www.giftbasketwholesalesupply.com/

3. http://www.giftbasketsupplies.com/Index.aspx?key=cat

4. http://www.americabasket.com/supplies.html

5. http://www.nashvillewraps.com/showpage.ww?page=giftbasket

6. http://www.giftbasketdropshipping.com/

7. http://www.buhiimports.com/index.html

8. http://www.dutchvalleyfoods.com/

9. http://www.naturesgardencandles.com/

10. http://www.ediblenature.com/

11. http://www.discountbeautycenter.com/

12. http://www.esutras.com/

Bonus Business Resource Web Sites

1. american merchandise liquidators

http://www.amlinc.com/

the closeout club

http://www.thecloseoutclub.com/

RJ discount sales

http://www.rjsks.com/

St louis wholesale

http://www.stlouiswholesale.com/

Wholesale Electronics

http://www.weisd.com/

ana wholesale

http://www.anawholesale.com/

office wholesale

http://www.1-computerdesks.com/

1aaa wholesale merchandise

http://www.1aaawholesalemerchandise.com/

big lots wholesale

http://www.biglotswholesale.com/

cmi computer

http://www.cmicomputer.com/

electronics

http://www.buy4lessinc.com/

computer dvds video games

http://www.compgallery.com/DYNAMIC/index.asp?CartId={CEEB7ED2-E0C6-4067-9A34-5E3F81F08C19}

overstock nation

http://www.overstocknation.com/

More Business Resources

2.   http://www.sba.gov/content/starting-green-business

home based businesses
3.   http://www.sba.gov/content/home-based-business

4.   online businesses
http://www.sba.gov/content/setting-online-business

5.   self employed and independent contractors
http://www.sba.gov/content/self-employed-independent-contractors

6.   minority owned businesses
http://www.sba.gov/content/minority-owned-businesses

7.   veteran owned businesses
http://www.sba.gov/content/veteran-service-disabled-veteran-owned

8.   woman owned businesses
http://www.sba.gov/content/women-owned-businesses

9.   people with disabilities
http://www.sba.gov/content/people-with-disabilities

10.   young entrepreneurs
http://www.sba.gov/content/young-entrepreneurs

BONUS MATERIAL

Incorporating your is the first step to asset protection. Below is a lot of fundamental information to incorporating your small business.

Incorporating a Small Business

Summary

If you are the owner-manager of a small business you may have been wondering about the advisability of incorporating your business, particularly if you are seeking equity capital.

This Management Aid does not discuss the advantages and disadvantages of the corporate form; its purpose is to acquaint you with some of the basic steps involved once you have decided to incorporate.

This Aid is not to be considered a substitute for professional advice. Legal guidance will insure that (a) the articles of incorporation and the bylaws are tailored to the needs of your particular business enterprise, (b) you understand the various aspects of the tax obligations involved, and (c) you will be in compliance with the State, local, and Federal laws affecting the corporation.

Laws governing the procedure for obtaining a corporate charter vary among States. Detailed information about the requirements of your State can be obtained from the secretary or other official designated to supervise the granting of corporate charters.

Choosing the Location

The majority of small and medium-sized businesses, especially those whose trade is local in nature, find it advisable to obtain their charter from the State in which the greatest part of their business is conducted.

Out-of-State, or "foreign," incorporation often results in the additional payments of taxes and fees in another jurisdiction.

Moreover, under the laws of many States the property of a foreign corporation is subject to less favorable treatment, especially in the area of attachment of corporate assets. This legal difference could prove especially hazardous to a small business.

On the other hand, you should look into possible benefits to be gained from incorporation in another State. Such factors as State taxes, restrictions on corporate powers and lines of business in which a company may engage, capital requirements, restrictions upon foreign corporations in your State, and so forth should be taken into consideration in selecting the State of incorporation.

For example, you should be aware that some States require a foreign corporation to obtain a certificate to do business in their State.

Without such certification the corporation may be deprived of the right to sue in those States.

The fee or organization tax charged for incorporation varies greatly from State to State.

Certificate Of Incorporation

Generally, the first step in the required procedure is preparation,

by the incorporators, of a "certificate of incorporation." Most

States used to require that the certificate be prepared by three or more legally qualified persons, but the modern trend is to require only one incorporator. An incorporator may, but not necessarily must, be an individual who will ultimately own stock in the corporation.

For purposes of expediting the filing of articles, "dummy" incorporators are often employed. These dummy incorporators are usually associated with a company that performs this service or with an attorney for the organizers. They typically elect their successors and resign at the meeting of the incorporators.

Many States have a standard certificate of incorporation form which may be used by small businesses. Copies of this form may be obtained from the designated State official who grants charters and, in some States, from local stationers as well. The following information is usually required:

1. The corporate name of the company. Legal requirements generally are (a) that the name chosen must not be so similar to the name of any other corporation authorized to do business in the State as to lead to confusion and (b) that the name chosen must not be deceptive so as to mislead the public. In order to be sure that the name you select is suitable, check out the availability of the name through the designated State official in each State in which you intend to do business before drawing up a certificate of incorporation. This check can be made through a service company. In some States, there is a procedure for reserving a name.

2. Purposes for which corporation is formed. Several States permit very broad language, such as "the purpose of the corporation is to engage in any lawful act or activity for which corporations may be organized." However, most States require more specific language in setting forth the purposes of the corporation. Even where State law does not require it, the better practice is to employ a "specific object" clause which spells out in broad descriptive terms the projected business enterprise. At the same time taking care to allow for the possibility of territorial, market, or product expansion.

In other words, the language should be broad enough to allow for expansion and yet specific enough to convey a clear idea of the projected enterprise.

The use of a specific object clause, even where not required by State law, is advisable for several reasons. It will convey to financial institutions a clearer picture of the corporate enterprise and will prevent problems in qualifying the corporation to do business in other jurisdictions. Reference books or certificates of existing corporations can provide examples of such clauses.

3. Length of time for which the corporation is being formed. This may be a period of years or may be perpetual.

4. Names and addresses of incorporators. In certain States one or more of the incorporators is required to be a resident of the State within which the corporation is being organized.

5. Location of the registered office of the corporation in the State of incorporation. If you decide to obtain your charter from another State, you will be required to have an office there. However, instead of establishing an office, you may appoint an agent in that State to act for you. The agent will be required only to represent the corporation, to maintain a duplicate list of stockholders, and to receive or reply to suits brought against the corporation in the State of incorporation.

6. Maximum amount and type of capital stock which the corporation wishes authorization to issue. The proposed capital structure of the corporation should be set forth, including the number and classification of shares and the rights, preferences, and limitations of each class of shares.

7. Capital required at time of incorporation. Some States require that a specified percentage of the par value of the capital stock be paid in cash and banked to the credit of the corporation before the certificate of incorporation is submitted to the designated State official for approval.

8. Provisions for preemptive rights, if any, to be granted to the stockholders and restrictions, if any, on the transfer of shares.

9. Provisions for regulation of the internal affairs of the corporation.

10. Names and addresses of persons who will serve as directors until the first meeting of stockholders or until their successors are elected and quality.

11. The right to amend, alter, or repeal any provisions contained in the certificate of incorporation. This right is generally statutory, reserved to a majority or two-thirds of the stockholders.

Still, it is customary to make it clear in the certificate.

If the designated State official determines that the name of the proposed corporation is satisfactory, that the certificate contains the necessary information and has been properly executed, and that there is nothing in the certificate or the corporation's proposed activities that violate State law or public policy, the charter will be issued.

Officers and Stockholders

Next, the stockholders must meet to complete the incorporation process. This meeting is extremely important. It is usually conducted by an attorney or someone familiar with corporate organizational procedure.

In the meeting the corporate bylaws are adopted and a board of directors is elected. This board of directors in turn will elect the officers who actually will have charge of the operations of the corporation--for example, the president, secretary, and treasurer. In small corporations, members of the board of directors frequently are elected as officers of the corporation.

Bylaws

The bylaws of the corporation may repeat some of the provisions of the charter and State statute but usually cover such items as the follows:

1. Location of the principal office and other offices of the corporation.

2. Time, place, and required notice of annual and special meetings of stockholders. Also the necessary quorum and voting privileges of the stockholders.

3. Number of directors, their compensation, their term of office, the method of electing them, and the method of creating or filling vacancies in the board of directors.

4. Time and place of the regular and special director's meetings, as well as the notice and quorum requirements.

5. Method of selecting officers, their titles, duties, terms of office, and salaries.

6. Issuance and form of stock certificates, their transfers and their control in the company books.

7. Dividends, when and by whom they may be declared.

8. The fiscal year, the corporate seal, the authority to sign checks, and the preparation of annual statement.

9. Procedure for amending the bylaws.

Special Tax Laws

At the time of the first meeting of the corporate board of directors and prior to issuance of any shares, you might consider adoption of a plan under a section of the Internal Revenue Code (IRC 1244) that grants ordinary rather than capital treatment of losses on certain "small business stock." Among the requirements of qualification as "section 1224 stock" are (1) the stock must be common stock, (2) the stock must be issued by the corporation for money or other property pursuant to a written plan containing several limitations, and (3) the amount of contribution received for the stock and equity capital of the corporation must not exceed maximum dollar limits.

You should be aware, also, of the possibility of electing subchapter S status (IRS 1371-1379). The purpose of subchapter S is to permit a "small business corporation" to elect to have its income taxed to the shareholders as if the corporation were a partnership. One objective is to overcome the double-tax feature of the present system of taxation of corporate income. Another purpose is to permit the shareholders to have the benefit of offsetting business losses by the corporation against the income of the shareholders.

Among the qualifying requirements for electing and maintaining "subchapter S" eligibility are that the corporation has no more than 10 shareholders, all of whom are individuals or estates; that there be no nonresident alien shareholders; that there be only one class of outstanding stock; that all shareholders consent to the election; and that a specified portion of the corporation's receipts be derived from actual business activity rather than passive investments. No limit is placed on the size of the corporation's income and assets.

If you plan to transfer property to a corporation in exchange for stock, you should realize that such a transfer is a taxable transaction unless the transfer complies with the provisions of IRC section 351.

Other Considerations

If your business is at present a sole proprietorship or partnership, you will need to secure a new taxpayer identification number and unemployment insurance account. You should find out in advance whether present licenses and leases will be transferable to the new corporate entity.

CREDIT REPAIR

INTRODUCTION

It is the purpose of this information is to teach you how to obtain a copy of your Consumer credit report and to remove such things as judgments, late payments, liens, or anything that is untrue orunfair from such reports, thereby improving your consumer credit rating.

WHAT IS CREDIT?

The average American has a better understanding of GeneralMotors than he or she does about their credit rating. Credit is used every day by millions of Americans, yet most do not have the faintest idea how our credit system really works. Most people only know that they can pull out a plastic credit card and buy something that they don't have the cash to pay for.

The dictionary defines credit as financial trustworthiness. Timegiven for payment for goods SOLD ON TRUST!

Actually, the credit system we now use is as old as the businessworld itself. The trend of today that we see advertisedeverywhere is: "BUY NOW AND PAY LATER." It is this philosophy that has caused millions of Americans to live from payday to payday, or from payment to payment!

Credit has been extended whenever goods are sold, or whereservices have been rendered and immediate payment of cash has NOT been made. The principle of credit is the same, whether the corner grocery store owner lets a patron "put it on the tab" until payday, or an executive takes a $5,000 cash advance from his American Express(TM) GOLD CARD!

What do you think would happen to the grocery store customer if when payday came around he DID NOT pay his bill as promised? Well, the grocer might give him more time, but chances are the grocer would no longer extend credit to such a customer. He would no longer be allowed to purchase his groceries "ON CREDIT!"

The same situation is true for the executive if he fails to payhis obligation for the $5,000 cash advance. His credit ratingwould be damaged, and that would make it very difficult for him to obtain a new credit card from American Express(TM) if he did not first clear up the debt that he owed.

With these examples in mind, if the grocer was stuck with a large unpaid bill, he would go around the neighborhood and tell all the other merchants that Mr. X "burned" him, and is NOT good credit risk. From that point on, none of the other merchants in town will give Mr. X any credit!

American Express(TM) would be faced with the very same problem. How would they inform other corporations that Mr. Executive is a poor credit risk? And how would American Express(TM) be able to obtain information on other clients who are applying for them for the credit for the first time?

The following pages will explain in more detail how credit is established and how you can investigate and improve your PERSONAL CREDIT REPORT. Be sure to read each sentence CAREFULLY as your credit is your FUTURE BUYING POWER. More important, your credit is your name!

Before you go on reading this information ask yourself one good question. How much is it worth to you to have GOOD CREDIT? The answer is simple. Good credit in our society is virtually "PRICELESS !" If your credit is not good, you will be severely handicapped in almost any financial endeavor you wish to accomplish. Because of these facts, the very small price which you paid for this financial report and credit guide is going to prove to be one of the best investments you've ever made!

Throughout this material we will show you a simple and legal way to develop a AAA credit reputation no matter what your past credit shows this very moment. Regardless of your present credit rating, whether it reflects no credit, slow credit, or simply bad credit, or EVEN if you filed bankruptcy... YOU CAN START AGAIN! You can be one of the more fortunate individuals in the

United States who holds GOOD CREDIT! You need it! You deserveit! And NOW you can have it!

HOW CREDIT REPORTING AGENCIES WORK

As credit increased throughout the country, there arose a great need to issue reports concerning those who are NOT a good credit risk as well as those who are CREDIT WORTHY! Because of this great need, credit reporting agencies were formed several years ago. These agencies, known as credit bureaus, receive information about consumers from banks, loan companies, creditcard companies, department stores, as well as from other credit and lending sources. Credit bureaus earn their profits by giving a computer printout showing a financial and credit profile of any individual (such as you or I). These reports are requested by a lender or an credit issuing firm from which you have requested credit.

Lenders will base their acceptance or rejection of your application for credit based on the information about you in your personal credit report. If your credit report shows that you have been reliable in the past, then in most cases credit will be granted. What if your report shows that you have NOT been reliable in the past? Perhaps you have been like others in this country who have encountered circumstances beyond your control which made it IMPOSSIBLE for you to meet your credit obligations. What if your credit report shows that you defaulted on a particular account or were constantly LATE making payments?

This of course can be most embarrassing, and usually leads to

CREDIT DENIAL!

There are over 2,500 credit reporting agencies in the United States. These agencies sell information about you to BANKS, DEPARTMENT STORES, CREDIT CARD COMPANIES, LOAN COMPANIES, etc.

These credit bureaus keep on file information concerning you and your credit, but they do not make any final judgements as to your credit worthiness. The decision is up to the lender whichyou have dealt with to decide and report to the credit bureau.

When you receive a copy of your credit profile, you may find some of the following information in your report. Your occupation, place of employment, income status, residence record, marital history, court and arrest records, and most important, details on payments of your past and present bills and loans.

You have the ABSOLUTE RIGHT to know what is in your consumer credit report! Because it is YOUR personal credit file, you should want to know what information the credit bureau is giving out concerning your good name and your credit!

Most people have thought, and still think, that if they have an unfavorable credit report or history that there is NO WAY to change it, and if they want to obtain NEW CREDIT that it's impossible! DON'T BELIEVE IT! You can change your credit report for the better. You can change and correct any and all OUTDATED, or INCORRECT INFORMATION that YOU choose! Remember, it's up to you! No one will do it for you! The first step in correcting information on your report is to obtain a copy of your personal credit profile.

HOW TO OBTAIN A COPY OF YOUR PERSONAL CREDIT REPORT

You have already learned how this credit information has been gathered, rated and placed on file for credit reporting. You can obtain a copy of this report just like a regular consumer would

- after all, it's your report.

-

There are many different credit reporting agencies in business today, and there is one in every community.

To evaluate your personal credit profile, you must obtain a copy of it.

You're entitled to one free copy of your credit report every 12 months from each of the three nationwide credit reporting companies. Order online from annualcreditreport.com, the only authorized website for free credit reports,

or call 1-877-322-8228..

THE FAIR CREDIT REPORTING ACT

The Fair Credit Reporting Act (FCRA) requires each of the nationwide credit reporting companies — Equifax, Experian, and TransUnion — to provide you with a free copy of your credit report, at your request, once every 12 months. The FCRA promotes the accuracy and privacy of information in the files of the nation's credit reporting companies. The Federal Trade Commission (FTC), the nation's consumer protection agency, enforces the FCRA with respect to credit reporting companies.

A credit report includes information on where you live, how you pay your bills, and whether you've been sued or have filed for bankruptcy. Nationwide credit reporting companies sell the information in your report to creditors, insurers, employers, and other businesses that use it to evaluate your applications for credit, insurance, employment, or renting a home.

Here are the details about your rights under the FCRA, which established the free annual credit report program.

Q: How do I order my free report?

The three nationwide credit reporting companies have set up a central website, a toll-free telephone number, and a mailing address through which you can order your free annual report.

To order, visit annualcreditreport.com, call 1-877-322-8228. Or complete the Annual Credit Report Request Form and mail it to: Annual Credit Report Request Service, P.O. Box 105281, Atlanta, GA 30348-5281. Do not contact the three nationwide credit reporting companies individually. They are providing free annual credit reports only through annualcreditreport.com, 1-877-322-8228 or mailing to Annual Credit Report Request Service.

You may order your reports from each of the three nationwide credit reporting companies at the same time, or you can order your report from each of the companies one at a time. The law allows you to order one free copy of your report from each of the nationwide credit reporting companies every 12 months.

A Warning About "Imposter" Websites

Only one website is authorized to fill orders for the free annual credit report you are entitled to under law — annualcreditreport.com. Other websites that claim to offer "free credit reports," "free credit scores," or "free credit monitoring" are not part of the legally mandated free annual credit report program. In some cases, the "free" product comes with strings attached. For example, some sites sign you up for a supposedly "free" service that converts to one you have to pay for after a trial period. If you don't cancel during the trial period, you may be unwittingly agreeing to let the company start charging fees to your credit card.

Some "imposter" sites use terms like "free report" in their names; others have URLs that purposely misspell annualcreditreport.com in the hope that you will mistype the name of the official site. Some of these "imposter" sites direct you to other sites that try to sell you something or collect your personal information.

Annualcreditreport.com and the nationwide credit reporting companies will not send you an email asking for your personal information. If you get an email, see a pop-up ad, or get a phone call from someone claiming to be from annualcreditreport.com or any of the three nationwide credit reporting companies, do not reply or click on any link in the message. It's probably a scam. Forward any such email to the FTC at spam@uce.gov.

Q: What information do I need to provide to get my free report?

A: You need to provide your name, address, Social Security number, and date of birth. If you have moved in the last two years, you may have to provide your previous address. To maintain the security of your file, each nationwide credit reporting company may ask you for some information that only you would know, like the amount of your monthly mortgage payment. Each company may ask you for different information because the information each has in your file may come from different sources.

Q: Why do I want a copy of my credit report?

A: Your credit report has information that affects whether you can get a loan — and how much you will have to pay to borrow money. You want a copy of your credit report to:

- make sure the information is accurate, complete, and up-to-date before you apply for a loan for a major purchase like a house or car, buy insurance, or apply for a job.
- help <u>guard against identity theft</u>. That's when someone uses your personal information — like your name, your Social Security number, or your credit card number — to commit fraud. Identity thieves may use your information to open a new credit card account in your name. Then, when they don't pay the bills, the delinquent account is reported on your credit report. Inaccurate information like that could affect your ability to get credit, insurance, or even a job.

Q: How long does it take to get my report after I order it?

A: If you request your report online at annualcreditreport.com, you should be able to access it immediately. If you order your report by calling toll-free 1-877-322-8228, your report will be processed and mailed to you within 15 days. If you order your report by mail using the Annual Credit Report Request Form, your request will be processed and mailed to you within 15 days of receipt.

Whether you order your report online, by phone, or by mail, it may take longer to receive your report if the nationwide credit reporting company needs more information to verify your identity.

Q: Are there any other situations where I might be eligible for a free report?

A: Under federal law, you're entitled to a free report if a company takes adverse action against you, such as denying your application for credit, insurance, or employment, and you ask for your report within 60 days of receiving notice of the action. The notice will give you the name, address, and phone number of the credit reporting company. You're also entitled to one free report a year if you're unemployed and plan to look for a job within 60 days; if you're on welfare; or if your report is inaccurate because of fraud, including identity theft. Otherwise, a credit reporting company may charge you a reasonable amount for another copy of your report within a 12-month period.

To buy a copy of your report, contact:

- Equifax:1-800-685-1111; equifax.com
- Experian: 1-888-397-3742; experian.com
- TransUnion: 1-800-916-8800; transunion.com

Q: Should I order a report from each of the three nationwide credit reporting companies?

A: It's up to you. Because nationwide credit reporting companies get their information from different sources, the information in your report from one company may not reflect all, or the same, information in your reports from the other two companies. That's not to say that the information in any of your reports is necessarily inaccurate; it just may be different.

Q: Should I order my reports from all three of the nationwide credit reporting companies at the same time?

A: You may order one, two, or all three reports at the same time, or you may stagger your requests. It's your choice. Some financial advisors say staggering your requests during a 12-month period may be a good way to keep an eye on the accuracy and completeness of the information in your reports.

Q: What if I find errors — either inaccuracies or incomplete information — in my credit report?

A: Under the FCRA, both the credit reporting company and the information provider (that is, the person, company, or organization that provides information about you to a consumer reporting company) are responsible for <u>correcting inaccurate or incomplete information in your report</u>. To take full advantage of your rights under this law, contact the credit reporting company and the information provider.

1. Tell the credit reporting company, in writing, what information you think is inaccurate.

Credit reporting companies must investigate the items in question — usually within 30 days — unless they consider your dispute frivolous. They also must forward all the relevant data you provide about the inaccuracy to the organization that provided the information. After the information provider receives notice of a dispute from the credit reporting company, it must investigate, review the relevant information, and report the results back to the credit reporting company. If the information provider finds the disputed information is inaccurate, it must notify all three nationwide credit reporting companies so they can correct the information in your file.

When the investigation is complete, the credit reporting company must give you the written results and a free copy of your report if the dispute results in a change. (This free report does not count as your annual free report.) If an item is changed or deleted, the credit reporting company cannot put the disputed information back in your file unless the information provider verifies that it is accurate and complete. The credit reporting company also must send you written notice that includes the name, address, and phone number of the information provider.

2. Tell the creditor or other information provider in writing that you dispute an item. Many providers specify an address for disputes. If the provider reports the item to a credit reporting company, it must include a notice of your dispute. And if you are correct — that is, if the information is found to be inaccurate — the information provider may not report it again.

Q: What can I do if the credit reporting company or information provider won't correct the information I dispute?

A: If an investigation doesn't resolve your dispute with the credit reporting company, you can ask that a statement of the dispute be included in your file and in future reports. You also can ask the credit reporting company to provide your statement to anyone who received a copy of your report in the recent past. You can expect to pay a fee for this service.

If you tell the information provider that you dispute an item, a notice of your dispute must be included any time the information provider reports the item to a credit reporting company.

Q: How long can a credit reporting company report negative information?

A: A credit reporting company can report most accurate negative information for seven years and bankruptcy information for 10 years. There is no time limit on reporting information about criminal convictions; information reported in response to your application for a job that pays more than $75,000 a year; and information reported because you've applied for more than $150,000 worth of credit or life insurance. Information about a lawsuit or an unpaid judgment against you can be reported for seven years or until the statute of limitations runs out, whichever is longer.

Q: Can anyone else get a copy of my credit report?

A: The FCRA specifies who can access your credit report. Creditors, insurers, employers, and other businesses that use the information in your report to evaluate your applications for credit, insurance, employment, or renting a home are among those that have a legal right to access your report.

Q: Can my employer get my credit report?

A: Your employer can get a copy of your credit report only if you agree. A credit reporting company may not provide information about you to your employer, or to a prospective employer, without your written consent.

For More Information

The FTC works for the consumer to prevent fraudulent, deceptive, and unfair business practices in the marketplace and to provide information to help consumers spot, stop, and avoid them. To file a complaint, visit ftc.gov/complaint or call 1-877-FTC-HELP (1-877-382-4357). The FTC enters Internet, telemarketing, identity theft, and other fraud-related complaints into Consumer Sentinel, a secure online database available to hundreds of civil and criminal law enforcement agencies in the U.S. and abroad.

Report Scams

If you believe you've responded to a scam, file a complaint with:

- the FTC
- your state Attorney General

You may wish to call your LOCAL credit bureau as well. Look in

your local yellow pages or go online and look under Credit Reporting Agencies.

Call up to find out mailing addresses and fees to obtain your report.

By the way, if you have been refused credit within the past 30 days and one of the reasons for the rejection was an "unfavorable" credit report, you have certain rights under the law.

You first have the right to know which credit reporting agency was used to obtain the report. You also have the right to CONTACT the agency and find out exactly what criteria on your report has caused the rejection You also have the right to obtain this information **FREE OF CHARGE** if you have been denied credit **WITHIN THE PAST 30 DAYS!**

Because with almost every important financial move that you make a credit report is involved, it is very important that you be concerned with what your credit report says regarding

YOU AND YOUR CREDIT!

HOW TO CORRECT ERRORS IN YOUR PERSONAL REPORT

After you have received your personal reports, determine the status of your credit file. You should attempt to remove ALL unfavorable information using the methods outlined herein.

Not all of your credit history is contained in either of the two firm's files. Some information may be duplicated, or not included in the other file. Your name and Social Security number are used for identification. Current and previous addresses, spouse's name, and date of birth are used for further identification. The credit information includes the merchants names, the subscriber number, credit account number, date opened, date closed, highest credit limit, highest amount of credit used, and repayment history. The last item is encoded into numbers, with a series of ones indicating perfect repayment.

After you have received your personal reports, determine the status of your credit file. You should attempt to remove ALL unfavorable information using the methods outlined herein.

The following descriptions are used to indicate payment history:

- Current Account - account open or closed in GOOD STANDING

- Inquiry - your credit information was requested by this firm or store

- Closed Account - credit account closed

- Paid Account - closed account or zero balance

- Credit Account Reinstated - previously closed account NOW AVAILABLE FOR USE

- Judgment - lawsuit against you... and NOT PAID

- Charge-Off - credit amount can not be collected

- Repossession - charged item returned to merchant

- Foreclosure - collateral sold to collect defaulted mortgage

- Collection Account - credit account assigned to collection agency

When you receive your report examine it VERY CAREFULLY. Make certain that all information is current and accurate. If you find any error (for example, a loan that you have PAID OFF is still listed as outstanding), you can take immediate action to correct the error. You must write out EXACTLY what the mistake is, and explain the way that the information SHOULD be listed.

For example, "Loan XYZ is NOT outstanding. It was paid in full on 10/31/2015." Send photocopies along with all pertinent information to substantiate your claim.

If you receive a computer printout of your credit file, there should be a space (Usually on the right-hand side of the report) in which you may PROTEST any item in your report that you feel is INCORRECT. After you have done this, make a photocopy, sending one copy back to the bureau by "CERTIFIED MAIL." When the credit bureau receives your report and the information in question, they are required to investigate and ADVISE YOU of the results of their investigation. There is NO CHARGE for this

investigation! YOU HAVE CREDIT RIGHTS! Due to the Fair Credit

Reporting Act passed in 1971!

Anytime that you are denied credit, you now have the right to know why you were turned down! If, for instance, you are turned down for a charge account at a store, you will receive a statement from the store stating that you were denied credit and their reason for the denial. If their reason has anything to do with the fact that the store used a credit reporting agency, they must provide you with the name and address of the agency that supplied them with the report. If this should happen to you, you should make an appointment within 30 days to visit the credit agency, so that you can review your report and find out what information in it is causing you to be DENIED CREDIT. I suggest that you always VISIT the credit bureau. Men should always wear a tie and jacket, and women should dress conservatively as well. It is very important to look professional and businesslike. It is also good to bring a friend along so that they can be witness whatever is said. Do not let the representative of the credit bureau confuse, or upset you in any way. If there is ANYTHING that you do not understand, ask to have it explained again.

If there is any information in that report that is not true, or if you want to dispute any information on it, don't be afraid to do so. If the agency is wrong on any item on your credit report or file, DEMAND a correction. By law, the company MUST investigate... many bureaus will even try to make the correction "on the spot?!"

If for some reason you cannot PROVE that the item is in error or if you are having a disagreement with a certain creditor, you have the RIGHT to tell your side of the story in 100 words or less! This will be ADDED to your report. Often, creditors who see that you have taken the time and effort to dispute an item in your credit file will NOT include it in credit worthiness.

This can be VERY HELPFUL to you.

Many bureau representatives will even help you word your statement. Be sure to use this rule to your ADVANTAGE!

After making any corrections on your report, you have the RIGHT to DEMAND that the credit bureau send corrected copies of your report to ALL CREDITORS who have received the incorrect reports for the LAST 6 MONTHS !

PLEASE NOTE: The credit bureaus WILL NOT do this automatically!

- ONLY WHEN ASKED! - So make sure it gets done PRONTO!

If, when looking over your report, you notice that it is missing a few POSITIVE items that you recall, you may want to invest some money to upgrade your report. Some credit bureaus will call creditors you name as FAVORABLE to you. If the information that you give turns out to be TRUE, the item will be ADDED to your report. There are sometimes small fees per item, but this small fee could be well worth it to you.

HOW TO ERASE "BAD CREDIT" FROM YOUR CREDIT REPORT

Past credit experience which shows delinquent payments, lawsuits, collection and bankruptcy is most definitely UNFAVORABLE on your credit report. Even with several other open accounts in good standing, the unfavorable information can be a cause of credit DENIAL when applying for new credit.

Incorrect and unverifiable information can be removed legally with the assistance of the credit reporting agency on whose files the unfavorable information appears. To do this you must contact the respective agency and tell them that you wish to dispute the particular information that you feel is injurious to your credit history. Legally, they must write for confirmation of the information to the source that is reporting it. If NO CONFIRMATION is received by the agency within 14 days... the information in question MUST BE DELETED from your file! - and an updated credit report will be mailed to you for verification!

Utilizing this method will eliminate most of the unfavorable information on your credit file, particularly that which is more than one year old, or if the disputed amount is under $500.

Any remaining information after the first attempt can usually be removed by subsequent attempts, at one month intervals. Remember, keep on trying over and over again -

PERSISTENCE DOES PAY OFF!

If there is any unfavorable information remaining on your credit file, you should add a statement to your file that DISPUTES this information. Remember, the credit agencies MUST add such a statement, PROVIDING YOU REQUEST IT! If possible, you may resolve the problem with the creditor in question. If so, have the creditor contact the credit agency FOR YOU.

How to Start a Gift Basket Business

(Video Training program)

http://goo.gl/bzGp1n

Made in the USA
Middletown, DE
26 February 2019